# Me and My Piano
## Part 1

with Fanny Waterman and Marion Harewood

My name is _____

I live at _____

_____

I had my first piano lesson on _____

My teacher's name is _____

FABER *ff* MUSIC

First published in 1988, 1989
by Faber Music Ltd.
This edition © 2019 by Faber Music Ltd.
Bloomsbury House
74–77 Great Russell Street
London WC1B 3DA
Music setting by Jeanne Roberts
Illustrated by Julia Osorno
Cover design by Lydia Merrills-Ashcroft
Page design by Susan Clarke
Printed in England by Caligraving Ltd
All rights reserved

ISBN10: 0-571-54150-X
EAN13: 978-0-571-54150-8

Dear _____

We are so glad you are going to learn to play the piano. The rainbow colours:

Red     Orange     Yellow     Green     Blue     Indigo     Violet

will help you to find the notes on the piano keyboard and on the music. In this book you'll meet

many new friends – Postman Pete, the Ostrich and his friends at the zoo, the Caterpillar and the

Old Man with the beard – as well as some old favourites such as Mary and her little lamb and

Old MacDonald. There are some exciting puzzles and games to work out, and when you finish

the book, your teacher will sign your certificate. We do hope that you and your piano will have

lots of fun together.

*Fanny Waterman and Marion Harewood*

## Teachers and parents

Note names are identified with colours to assist note learning. Matching coloured stickers on the piano keys may be found helpful in the early stages. It is important to say the words of each piece aloud before playing it, as this will help with the rhythm.

2

Crossword solution  Across: 4 Semibreve; 5 Bass; 6 Crescendo; 10 Softer   Down: 1 Minims; 2 Treble; 3 Keys; 4 Staccato; 7 Clef; 8 Note; 9 One

# Always

- Play with clean hands and short fingernails.

- Check that the chair or piano stool is in the middle of the keyboard and at the right height.

- Make sure you are sitting correctly, with a straight back.

- Play with curved fingers, like this:

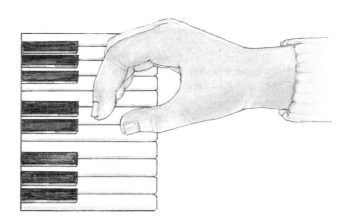

- Use the same fingering every time you play a piece. This will help you to play from memory.

- Every note you play on the piano should be beautiful. Listen carefully.

# The piano keyboard

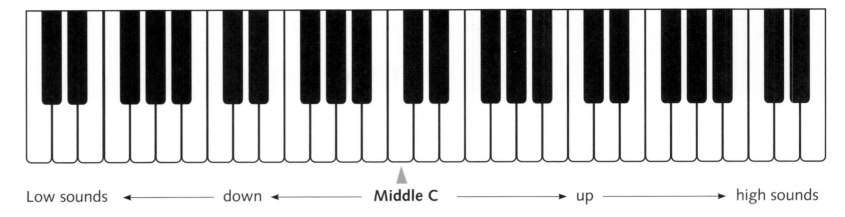

Low sounds ← down ← **Middle C** → up → high sounds

The piano keyboard has **white** and **black** notes.
The **black** notes are in groups of twos and threes.

Find the group of two **black** notes nearest to the middle.
The **white** note to the left of them is called **Middle C**.

Imagine you are a frog hopping up the keyboard.

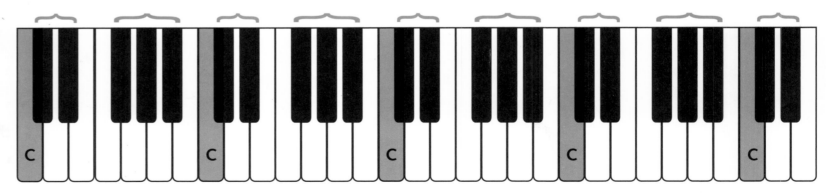

Look for all the C notes on the keyboard.
Then play every C note from the bottom to the top, hopping like a frog from one to the next.
Start with the left hand, changing to the right hand at middle C.

# The musical rainbow

The musical alphabet has seven letters, just as the rainbow has seven colours. These seven letters are repeated all the way up the piano keyboard.

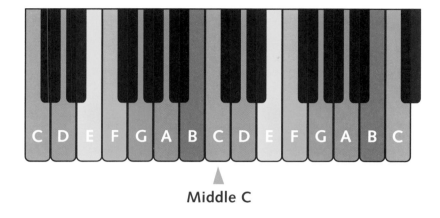

Middle C

## Find Middle C

From Middle C, climb up the musical rainbow, naming each note aloud as you go. At the top, play another C, then climb back down, naming each note. Now you have played an octave. Use any finger you like.

## Frog hops

Play every D from the bottom to the top. Then every E, then F, G, A and B. Now you are back to C!

## Three blind mice

Here are the first notes of *Three blind mice*:
**E D C**, **E D C**, **G F E**, **G F E**.
Play them on the piano.

## Word game

Can you play these words?

**BAG**　　**CAB**　　**BEE**　　**BED**　　**FACE**

# Counting the time

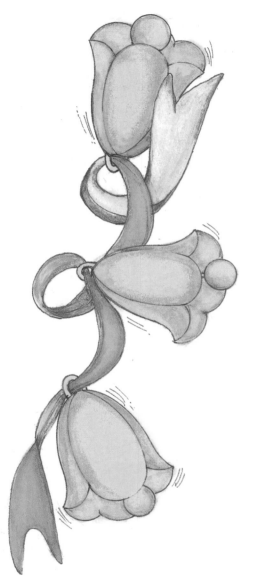

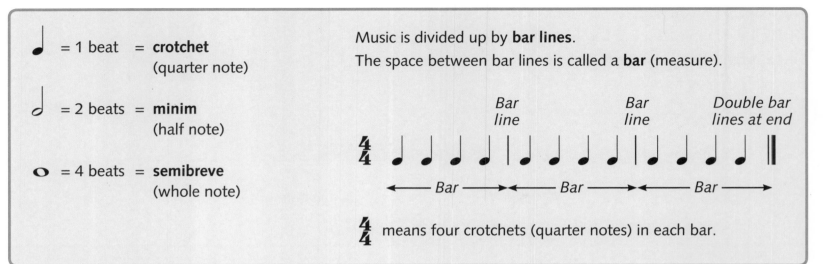

♩ = 1 beat = **crotchet**
(quarter note)

𝅗𝅥 = 2 beats = **minim**
(half note)

○ = 4 beats = **semibreve**
(whole note)

Music is divided up by **bar lines**.
The space between bar lines is called a **bar** (measure).

$\frac{4}{4}$ means four crotchets (quarter notes) in each bar.

Clap these rhythms, counting aloud to four. The notes marked > should have an **accent**.
Play them louder than the others.

**Teacher**
Turn these into duets
by clapping crotchets.

> Say the words aloud, clapping the time.
>
> Now say the words again, playing Middle C at the same time.

## Yankee doodle

Yan - kee Doo - dle went to town rid - ing on a po — ny.

Stuck a fea - ther in his hat and called it MA - CA - RO — NI.

## Sing a song of sixpence

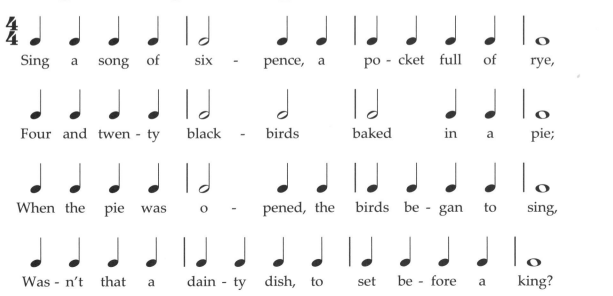

Sing a song of six - pence, a po - cket full of rye,

Four and twen - ty black - birds baked in a pie;

When the pie was o - pened, the birds be - gan to sing,

Was - n't that a dain - ty dish, to set be - fore a king?

# Finding your way from the music

1. Music is written on a **stave** or **staff**.
   It has five lines with four spaces in between.

2. Notes are written on the **lines** or in the **spaces**.

   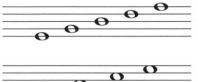

3. High notes are written in the **treble clef**.
   (Right hand.)

   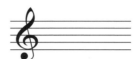

4. **Middle C** has its very own line.
   In the treble clef it is **below** the stave.

5. The right hand plays high notes.

   **Hold up your right hand.**
   Point to your 3rd finger.
   Point to your 1st finger.
   Point to your 5th finger.
   Point to your 2nd finger.
   Point to your 4th finger.

   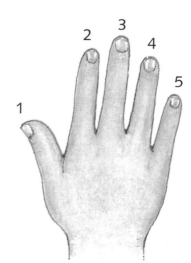

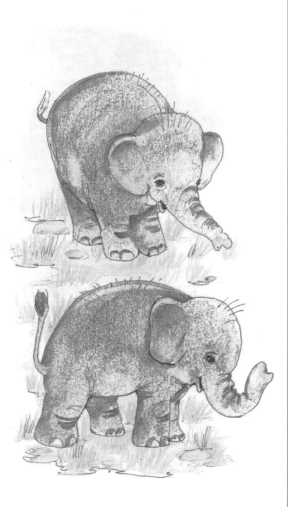

# Going to the zoo

Say the words, clap the rhythm, then play.

## Kangaroo

We are go - ing to the zoo. We will see a kan - ga - roo.

**new note**

## C

New note C

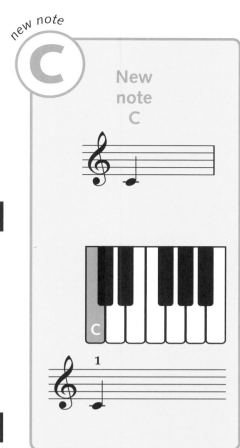

## Crocodile

Cro - co - dile, How you smile, If you move I'll run a mile.

## Bears

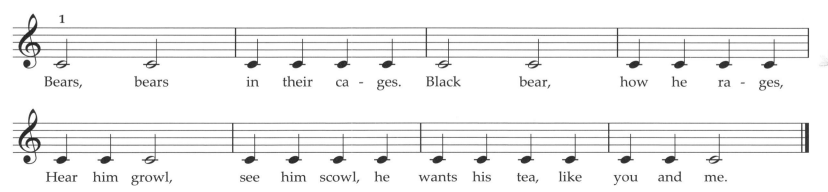

Bears, bears in their ca - ges. Black bear, how he ra - ges,

Hear him growl, see him scowl, he wants his tea, like you and me.

## New note D

New
note
D

## Middle D, Middle C

Mid - dle   D.     Mid - dle   C.     Green  and  blue  are   D   and   C.

## Postman Pete

Post - man  Pete      has   big  feet.      Hear  him  com - ing   down  the  street.

Knock, knock, knock,    on   our  door.     There's  a   let - ter   on   the  floor.

**Postman Pete** *accompaniment*

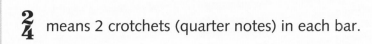

$\frac{2}{4}$ means 2 crotchets (quarter notes) in each bar.

## At the piano

Let's be - gin my mu - sic les - son, I can now play C D C.

## My pony

Trot - ting on my po - ny, She's a lit - tle dap - ple grey.

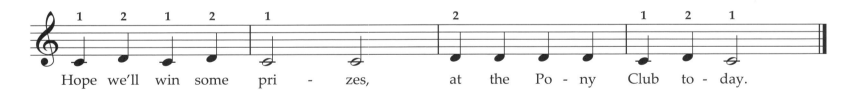

Hope we'll win some pri - zes, at the Po - ny Club to - day.

**My pony** *accompaniment*

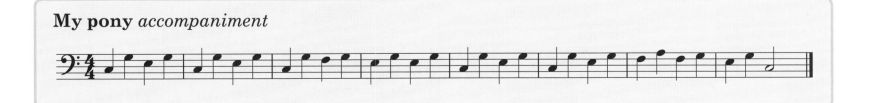

**11**

New note D

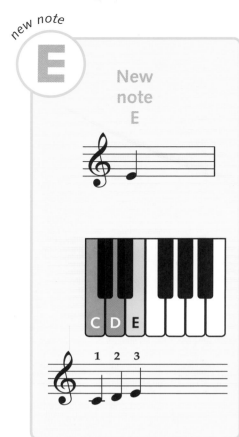

*new note*

# E

New note E

## This is E

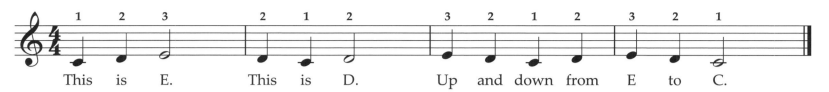

1   2   3    2   1   2    3   2   1   2    3   2   1

This   is   E.    This   is   D.    Up   and   down   from   E   to   C.

This sign ‖ at the end of a piece is a **repeat sign**. It means play the piece again.

## Telephone

3       2       3    2       3   2   1

1. Te - le - phone.    It's   for   me.    Grand-ma's   ask - ing   us   to   tea.
2. We'll   have   chips,    we'll   have   cake,    We'll   have   ice - cream   on   a   plate.

**Telephone** *accompaniment*

New note E

# Sammy squirrel

Sam - my squir - rel up a tree, Climbs the bran - ches ea - si - ly.

Sam - my, please come down the tree, back to me.

# The ostrich

**Fingering**

Use next-door fingers for next-door notes.
A note left out means a finger left out.

A dot after a note increases its length by half.

♩. = 3 beats = **dotted minim** (dotted half note) (𝅗𝅥 + ♩)

*Words by May Wilkins Freer*

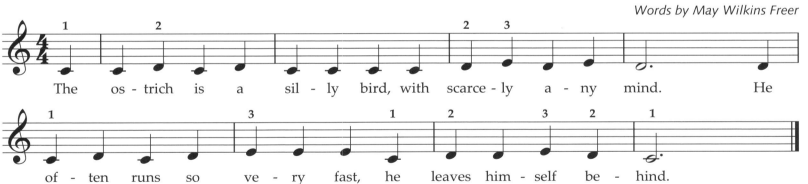

The os - trich is a sil - ly bird, with scarce - ly a - ny mind. He

of - ten runs so ve - ry fast, he leaves him - self be - hind.

**Sammy squirrel** and **The ostrich** *accompaniment*

new note

**New note F**

## Good night, good morning

Close your eyes for the night. We will wake up when it's light.

## Snowflakes

Snow-flakes gent - ly swirl - ing round, fall - ing soft - ly to the ground.

**Good night, good morning** *accompaniment*

**Snowflakes** *accompaniment*

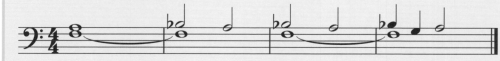

New note F

Tunes can start on any beat of the bar. This one starts on the 4th beat.

# The railway train

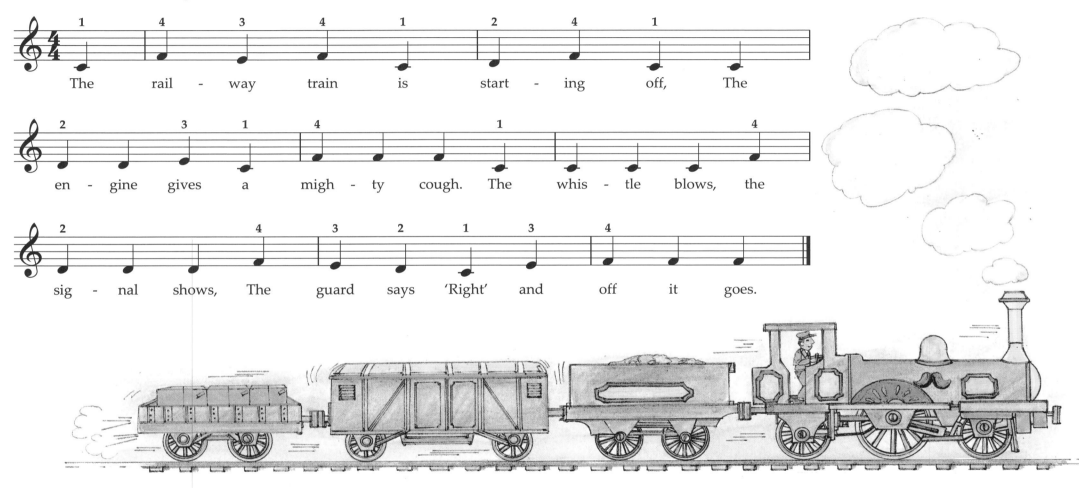

The rail - way train is start - ing off, The
en - gine gives a migh - ty cough. The whis - tle blows, the
sig - nal shows, The guard says 'Right' and off it goes.

**The railway train** *accompaniment*

New note F

New note G

# Escalator

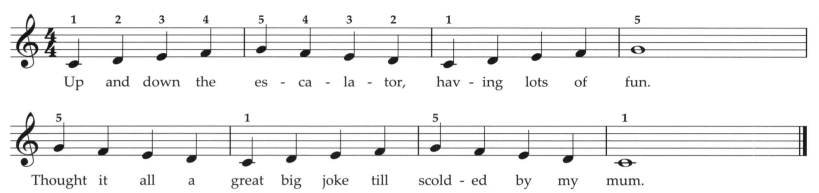

Up and down the es - ca - la - tor, hav - ing lots of fun.

Thought it all a great big joke till scold - ed by my mum.

# Jelly on a plate

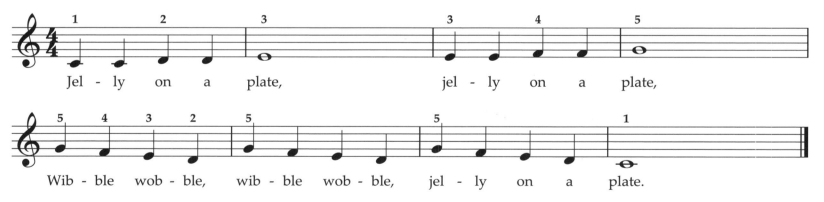

Jel - ly on a plate, jel - ly on a plate,

Wib - ble wob - ble, wib - ble wob - ble, jel - ly on a plate.

**Jelly on a plate** *accompaniment*

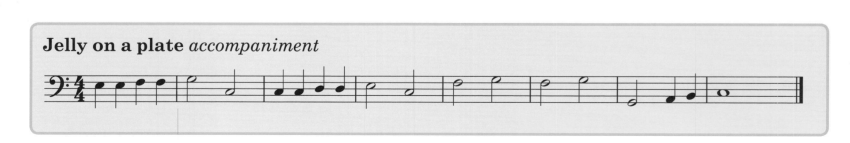

New note G

# The pancake

Words by Christina Rossetti

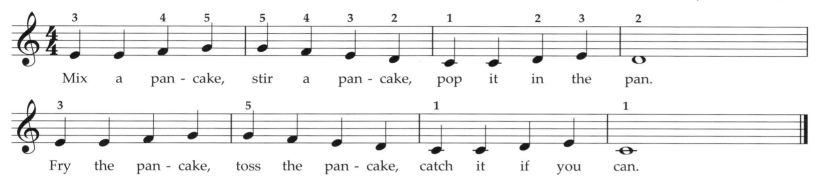

Mix a pan-cake, stir a pan-cake, pop it in the pan.

Fry the pan-cake, toss the pan-cake, catch it if you can.

# Mary had a little lamb

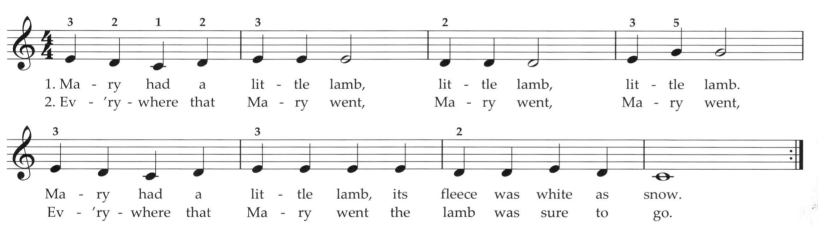

1. Ma - ry had a lit - tle lamb, lit - tle lamb, lit - tle lamb.
2. Ev - 'ry - where that Ma - ry went, Ma - ry went, Ma - ry went,

Ma - ry had a lit - tle lamb, its fleece was white as snow.
Ev - 'ry - where that Ma - ry went the lamb was sure to go.

**The pancake** *accompaniment*

**Mary had a little lamb** *accompaniment*

**17**

New note G

# Three in a bar

> **3/4** means 3 crotchets (quarter notes) in each bar.

Clap these rhythms, counting aloud to 3.

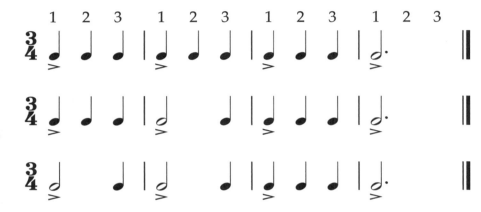

**Teacher**
Turn these into duets by clapping crotchets.

# Humpty Dumpty

Clap the time, saying the words aloud.

Hump - ty Dump - ty sat on a wall.

Hump - ty Dump - ty had a great fall.

All the king's hor - ses and all the king's men

Could - n't put Hump - ty to - ge - ther a - gain.

## Dynamics (loud and soft)

$f$ = *forte* = **loud**     $p$ = *piano* = **soft**

# Little Bo-Peep

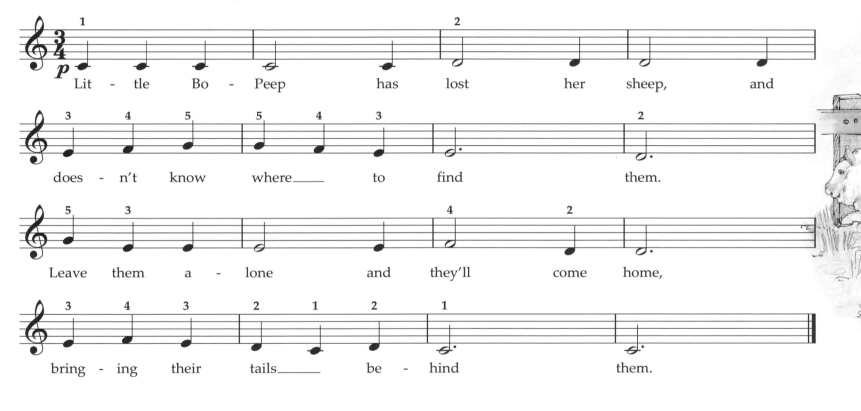

Lit - tle Bo - Peep has lost her sheep, and

does - n't know where___ to find them.

Leave them a - lone and they'll come home,

bring - ing their tails___ be - hind them.

**Little Bo-Peep** *accompaniment*

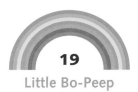

# Monkey puzzles 1

**Write in the name of these notes:**

**Write these notes on the stave, then play them:**

C   G   D   F   E        C   D   E   F   G        D   F   C   D   E

**Add the bar lines to these tunes:**

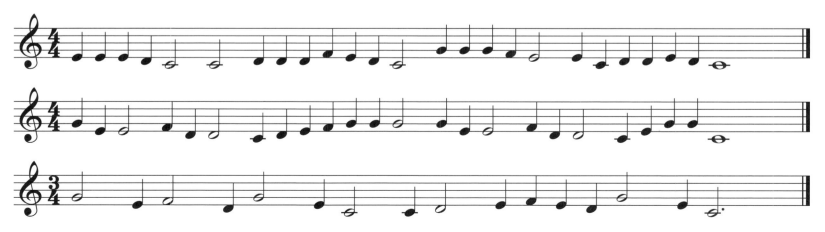

**Play these words:**

F E D    E G G    E D G E

**Copy these treble clefs:**

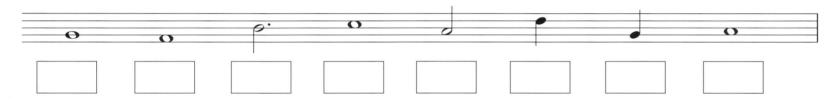

| = 1 beat = crotchet (quarter note) |
| = 2 beats = minim (half note) |
| = 3 beats = dotted minim (dotted half note) |
| = 4 beats = semibreve (whole note) |

**How many beats in each note?**

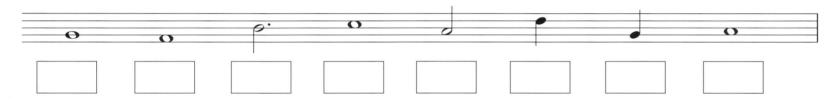

**How many beats to each bar?**

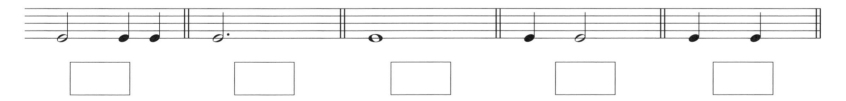

**Write these notes:**

semibreve G      minim D      dotted minim F      crotchet C      minim E

# Girls and boys come out to play

**f** Girls and boys come out to play, the
moon doth shine——— as bright as day.
Leave your sup - pers and leave your sleep, and
come with your play - fel - lows in the street.

**Girls and boys** *accompaniment*

# The left hand

1 Low notes are written in the bass clef. (Left hand.)

2 Middle C has its own line.
In the bass clef, it is **above** the stave.

3 The left hand plays low notes.

**Hold up your left hand:**
Point to your 3rd finger.
Point to your 1st finger.
Point to your 5th finger.
Point to your 2nd finger.
Point to your 4th finger.

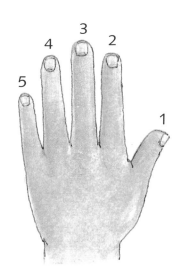

## Left hand Middle C

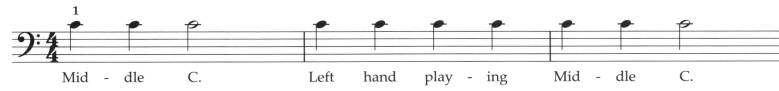

Mid - dle C. Left hand play - ing Mid - dle C.

## B

New note B

Left hand C

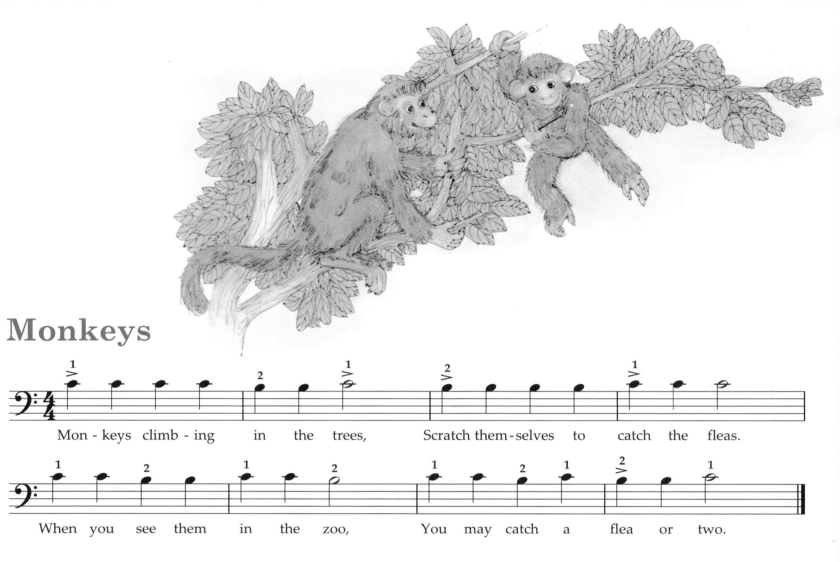

## Monkeys

Mon - keys climb - ing    in    the    trees,    Scratch them - selves    to    catch    the    fleas.

When    you    see    them    in    the    zoo,    You    may    catch    a    flea    or    two.

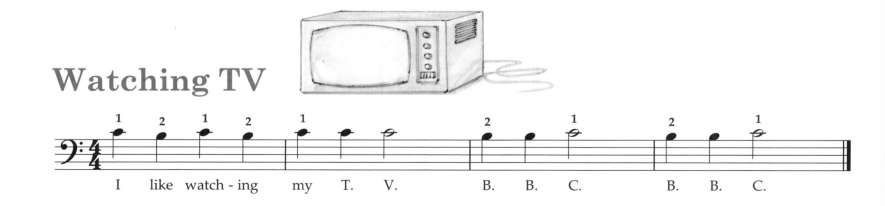

## Watching TV

I    like    watch - ing    my    T.    V.    B.    B.    C.    B.    B.    C.

New note B

# The caterpillar

Ca - ter - pil - lar crawl - ing round. His 8 feet make not a sound.

# What is your name?

What is your name? Gem - ma or Jane?

Don't tell me now, I'll ask you a - gain.

**The caterpillar** *accompaniment*

**What is your name?** *accompaniment*

New note B

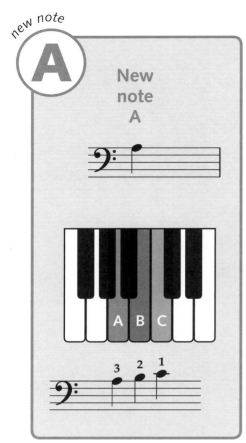

## New note A

# Ladybird

La - dy - bird, la - dy - bird, fly a - way home. Your

house is on fire and your chil - dren are gone.

# Marching

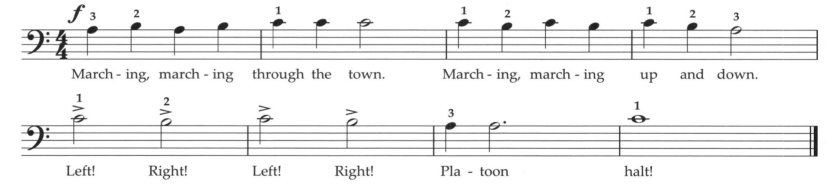

March - ing, march - ing through the town. March - ing, march - ing up and down.

Left! Right! Left! Right! Pla - toon halt!

**Ladybird** *accompaniment*

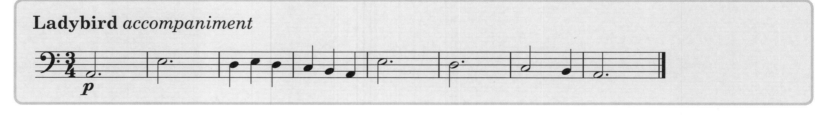

**Marching** *accompaniment*

# Oh dear me!

Oh dear me! I'm not tall.

I can't catch my bounc - ing ball.

# Who's that knocking?

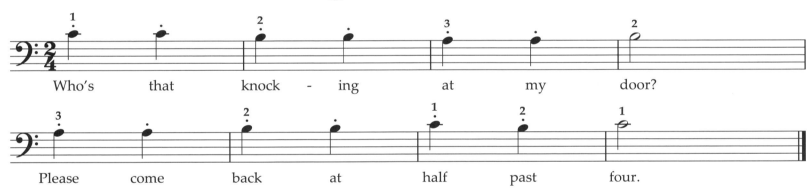

Who's that knock - ing at my door?

Please come back at half past four.

## Staccato

A dot placed over or under a note makes it short and crisp. Play with a loose wrist like a bouncing ball.

**Oh dear me!** *accompaniment*

**Who's that knocking?** *accompaniment*

**27**

New note A

new note

**G**

New note
G

## This is C, this is G

This    is    C,        this    is    G,        C    G    C    G    back    to    C.

## The squirrel

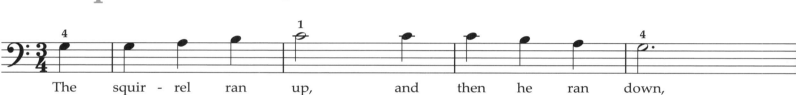

The    squir - rel    ran    up,        and    then    he    ran    down,

Up    a - gain,    down    a - gain,    then    round    and    round.

**The squirrel** *accompaniment*

mp = *mezzo piano* = **moderately soft**

mf = *mezzo forte* = **moderately loud**

# I am the Prince

I    am    the    Prince,        hap - py    and    free.

This    is    a    waltz,        come    dance    with    me.

**I am the Prince** *accompaniment*

**29**

New note G

New note F

## Running down to F

Run - ning  down  to  F  and  back  to  C  G  C.

## See-saw

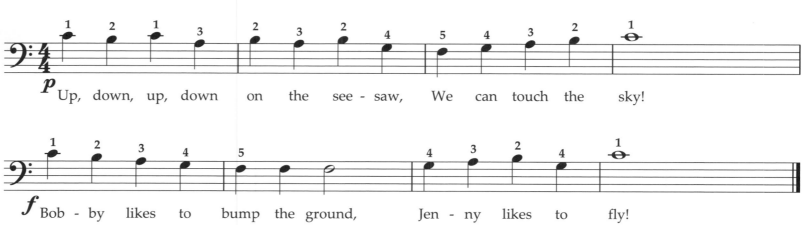

*p* Up,  down,  up,  down  on  the  see - saw,  We  can  touch  the  sky!

*f* Bob - by  likes  to  bump  the  ground,  Jen - ny  likes  to  fly!

# The robin

Lit - tle ro - bin red - breast sat up - on a tree.

When I threw him bread - crumbs, he flew down to me.

# Bugle call

Ta - ra ta - ra boom - de - ay, Hear the bu - gle call to - day.

New note F

# Two hands

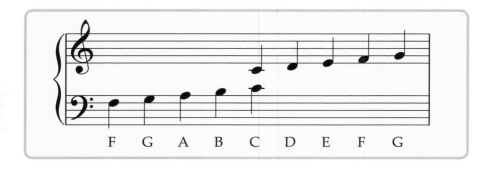

F G A B C D E F G

## The spaceman

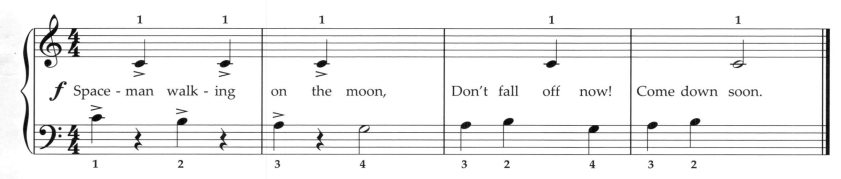

*f* Space - man walk - ing | on the moon, | Don't fall off now! | Come down soon.

## Westminster chimes

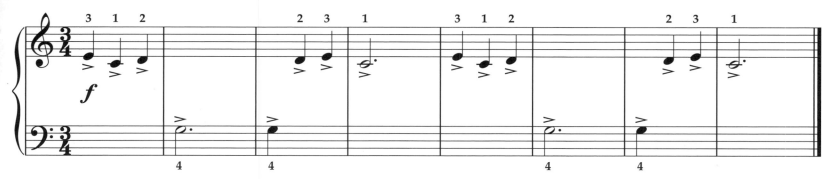

**Teacher** Now play the chord:

# Jungle drums

crescendo
= **getting louder**

decrescendo
or diminuendo
= **getting softer**

# Rowing

If two notes of the same pitch are joined by a curve

or

this is called a **TIE**.

Play the first note and hold it on for the value of the second note.

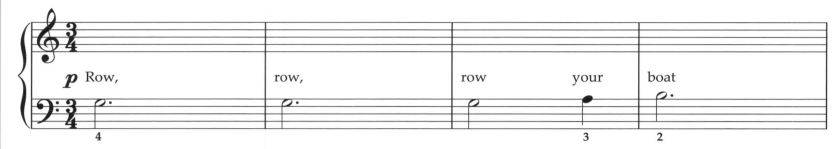

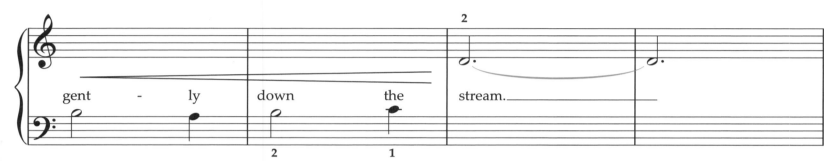

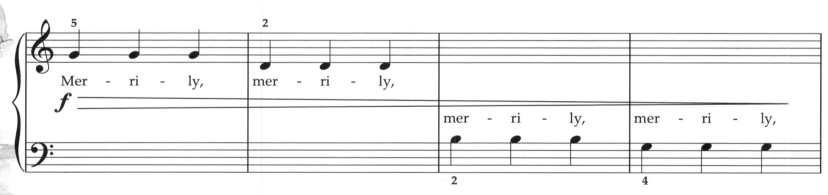

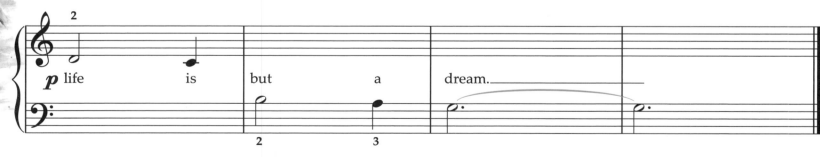

# Pussy cat

*p* Pus - sy cat, pus - sy cat, where have you been? I've

been up to Lon - don to vi - sit the Queen.

*p* Pus - sy cat, pus - sy cat, what did you there? I

fright - ened a lit - tle mouse un - der her chair. *Mee - ow.*

# Monkey puzzles 2

**Write in these notes:**

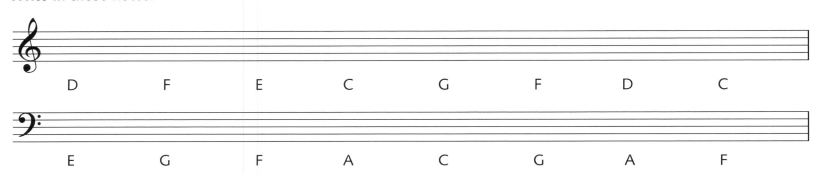

D    F    E    C    G    F    D    C

E    G    F    A    C    G    A    F

**Copy more bass clefs:**

## A musical crossword

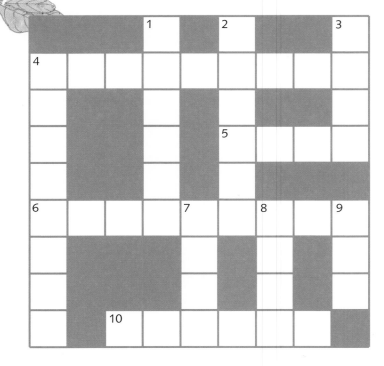

*Across*

4  Note with 4 beats.
5  The clef for the left hand.
6  Getting louder.
10 *Diminuendo* means getting ……

*Down*

1  Notes with 2 beats.
2  The clef for the right hand.
3  They're black and white.
4  The name for dots over the notes.
7  The sign at the beginning of a stave.
8  Middle C (or D or E) is a …?
9  The number of the finger you would
   use to play C in either hand.

*Answers on page 2*

**Quiz**

Write your answers in the spaces and then play them on the piano.

Where you go to sleep ___ ___ ___

Hard of hearing ___ ___ ___ ___                 A green vegetable ___ ___ ___ ___ ___ ___ ___

A furry insect that stings ___ ___ ___          A father ___ ___ ___

A lot of these make a necklace ___ ___ ___ ___   What Humpty Dumpty was ___ ___ ___

Can you make up some more words on the piano?

# Yankee Doodle

1  Fill in the missing notes marked * with their proper time values.
2  Put in the bar lines.
3  Now play **Yankee Doodle**.

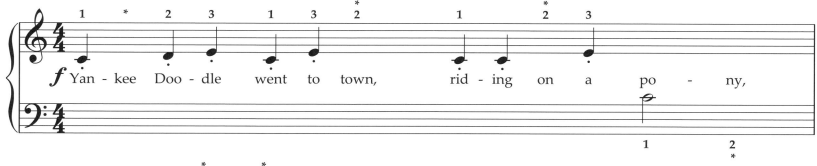

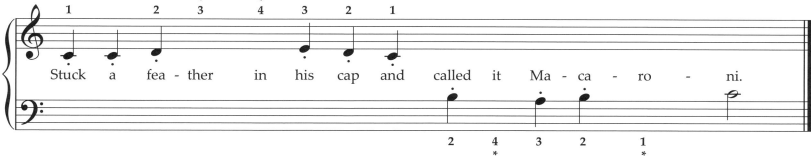

# Rests

| Crotchet rest | Minim rest | Semibreve rest |
|---|---|---|
| (quarter-note rest) | (half-note rest) | (whole-note rest) |
|  |  |  |
| One silent beat | Two silent beats (sitting on the third line) | Four silent beats or a whole bar's rest even in $\frac{3}{4}$ time (hanging from the second line) |

Clap the notes, counting the beats aloud.

# Old MacDonald

# A carol for Christmas
## We three kings

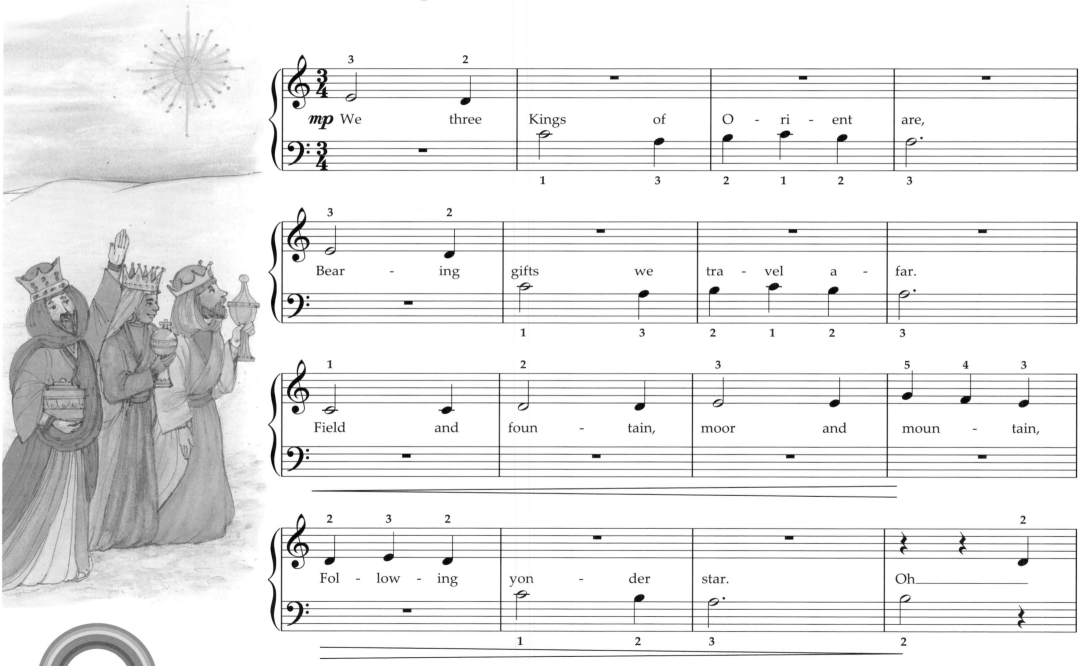

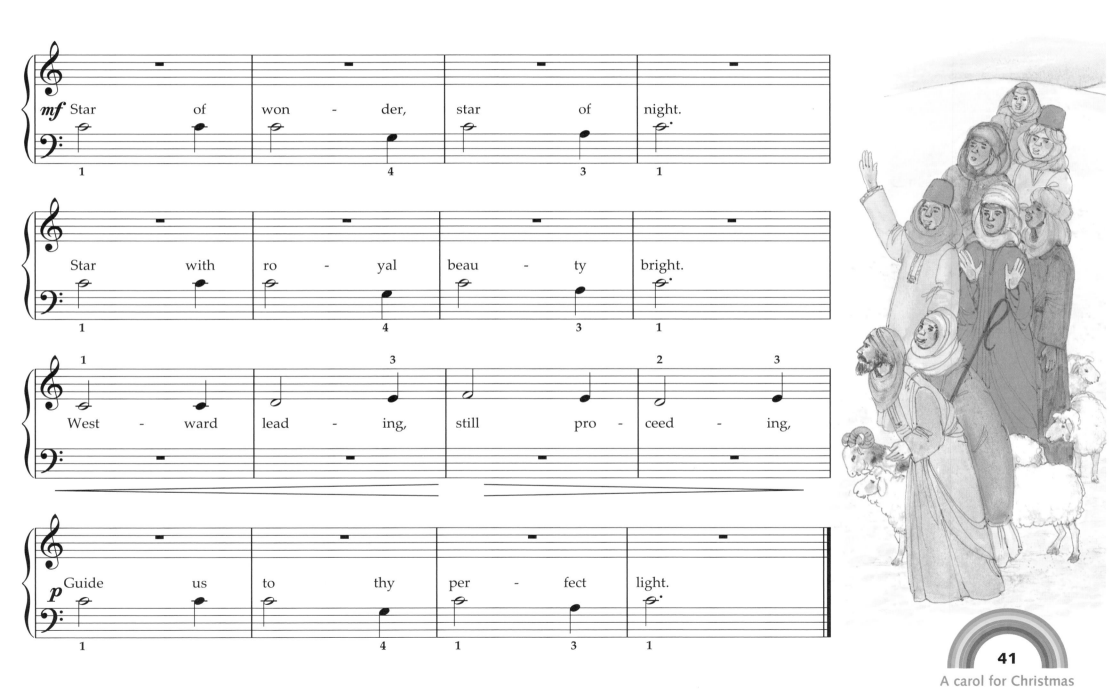

A carol for Christmas

# The laughing clown

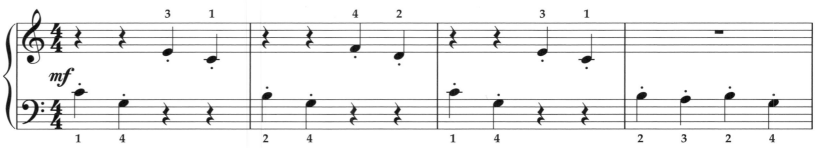

## Musical detective

1 How many bars are there in the piece? How many beats in each bar?
2 What do the dots under the notes mean?
3 How many crotchet rests are there?
4 How many notes does the left hand play?
5 Is the piece loud, moderately loud or soft?
6 Make up your own words for the piece.

# My clock

# Down by the lakeside

*Music by Beethoven*

Hands together

# Oh when the Saints go marching in

*American traditional*

**In march style**

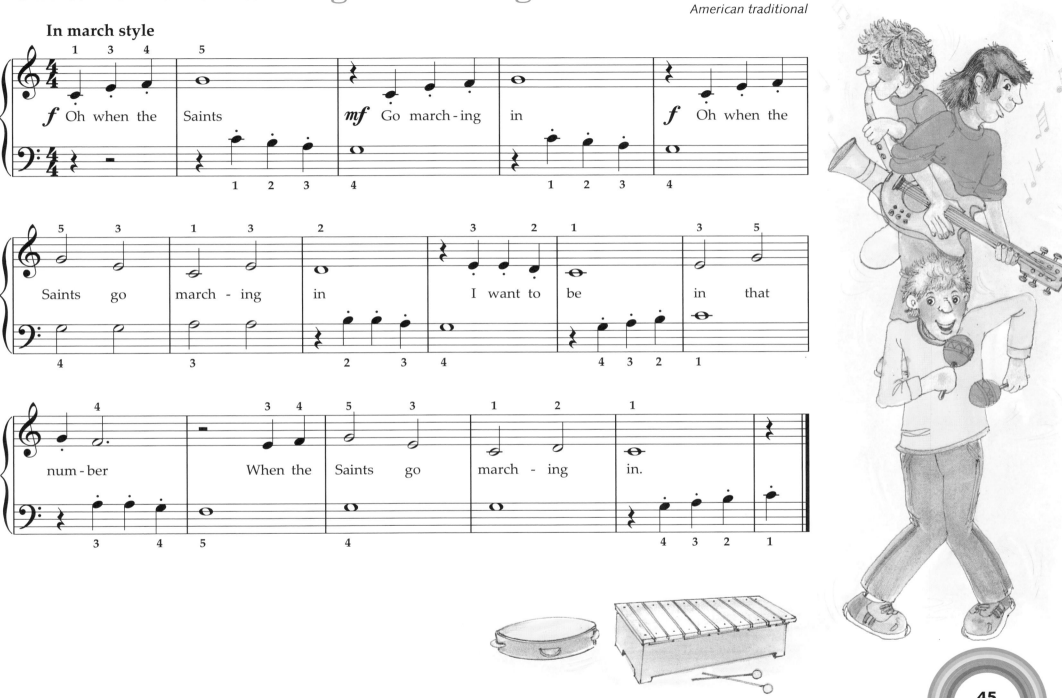

f Oh when the Saints Go march-ing in f Oh when the

Saints go march - ing in I want to be in that

num - ber When the Saints go march - ing in.

# The haunted castle

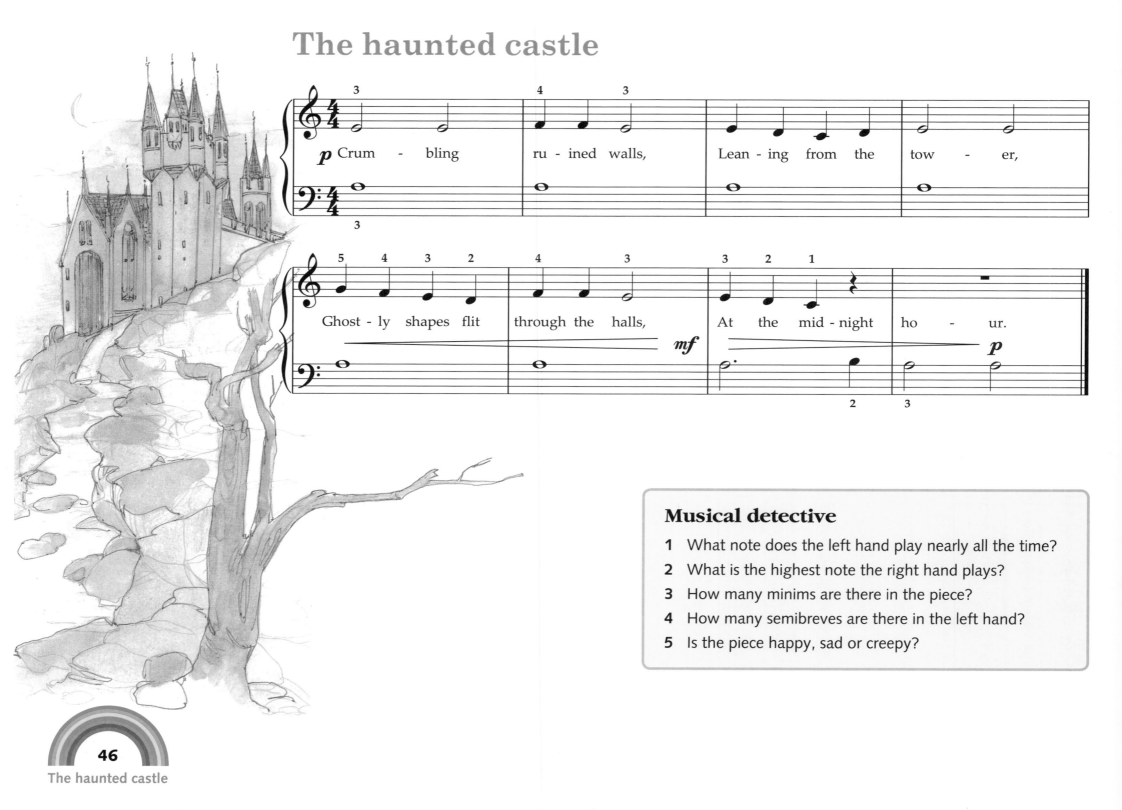

## Musical detective

1  What note does the left hand play nearly all the time?
2  What is the highest note the right hand plays?
3  How many minims are there in the piece?
4  How many semibreves are there in the left hand?
5  Is the piece happy, sad or creepy?

# There was an old man with a beard

*Words by Edward Lear*

*mf* There was an Old Man with a be - ard *f* Who

said, 'It is just as I fe - ared *p* Two

owls and a hen, Four larks and a wren *f* Have

all built their nests in my be - ard'.

# Rainbow certificate

This is to certify that

_____

successfully completed

## Me and My Piano Part 1

on _____

## Congratulations!

*Fanny Waterman.*
*Fanny Waterman*

*Marion Harewood*
*Marion Harewood*

_____

*Teacher's signature*

To Alexandra, Carmella and Gemma

# Me and My Piano
## Part 2

### with Fanny Waterman and Marion Harewood

My name is _____

I live at _____

_____

I started this book on _____

My teacher's name is _____

FABER *ff* MUSIC

Hello _____

Here's another piano book with lots of pieces and puzzles for you to enjoy. We should like to introduce you to some new friends – the Zebra, the Crooked Man, the Lady of Niger and her hungry Tiger, the Grasshopper and the Elephant, and many more colourful characters.

Have you seen your own shadow? Footsteps in the snow? Bonfires in the autumn? Moon and stars? You will if you learn to play the pieces in this book. Try to get a star for each lesson. Ten stars deserve a small prize from your teacher or parent!

Have fun!

*Fanny Waterman and Marion Harewood*

## Star chart

_____ ☐ ☐ ☐          _____ ☐ ☐ ☐

_____ ☐ ☐ ☐          _____ ☐ ☐ ☐

_____ ☐ ☐ ☐          _____ ☐ ☐ ☐

_____ ☐ ☐ ☐          _____ ☐ ☐ ☐

_____ ☐ ☐ ☐          _____ ☐ ☐ ☐

# The musical alphabet

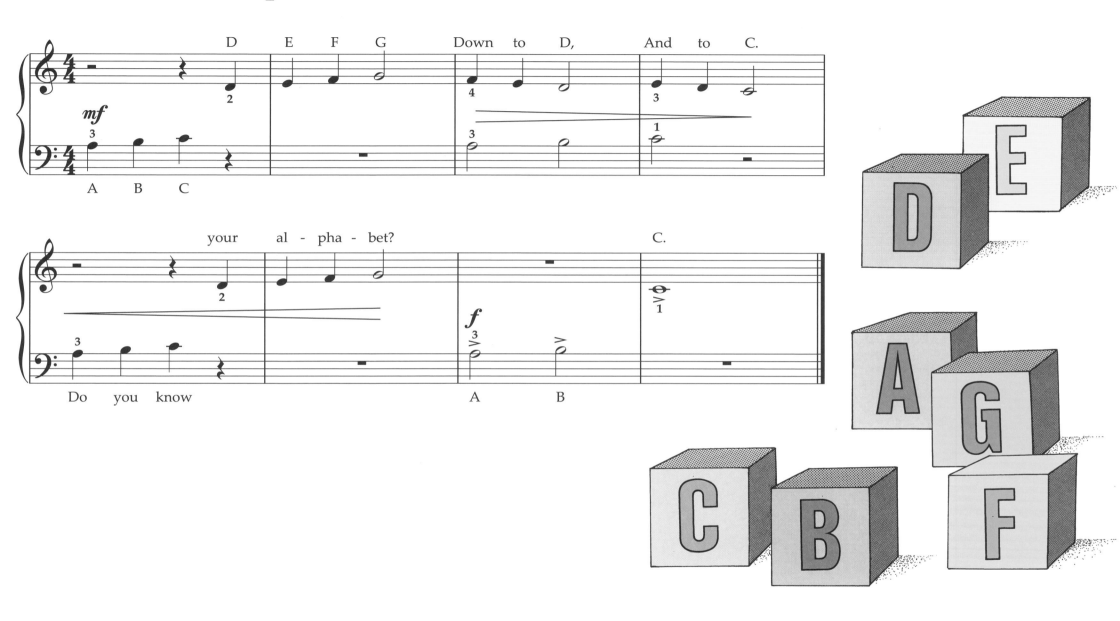

# My black cat

My black cat is ve - ry fat, I give him milk to drink, And

when I ask 'Is that e - nough?' He an - swers with a wink.

# The zebra

*Words by Edward Lear*

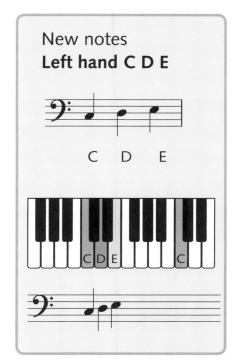

**New notes**
**Left hand C D E**

C D E

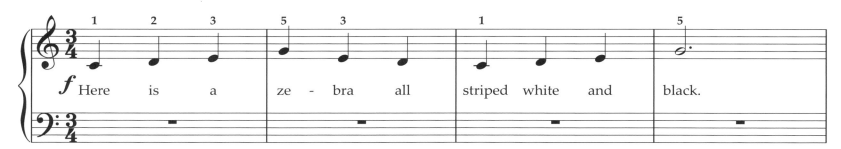

*f* Here is a ze - bra all striped white and black.

*mf*

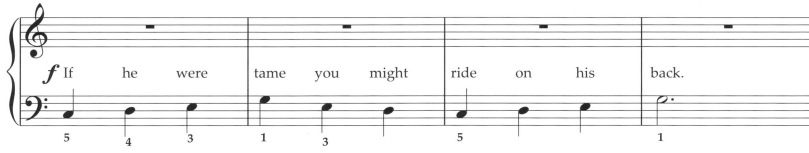

*f* If he were tame you might ride on his back.

*mf*

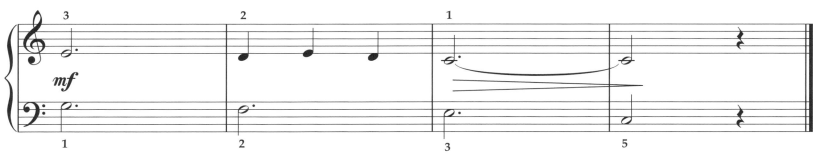

**53**
New notes LH C, D, E

## The slur
## Legato

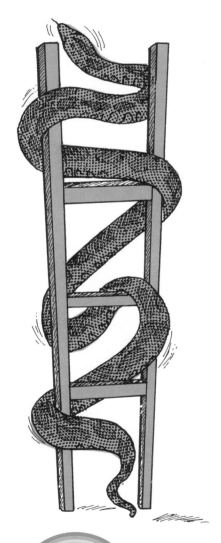

Notes covered by a **slur** should be played smoothly (**legato**).
Think of them as being under the cover of an umbrella.

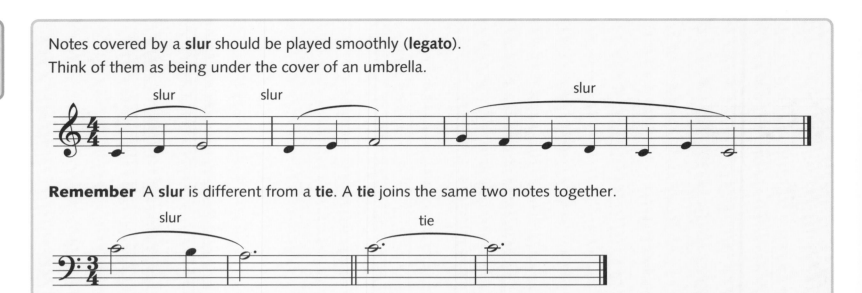

**Remember** A **slur** is different from a **tie**. A **tie** joins the same two notes together.

# Snakes and ladders

# There was a crooked man

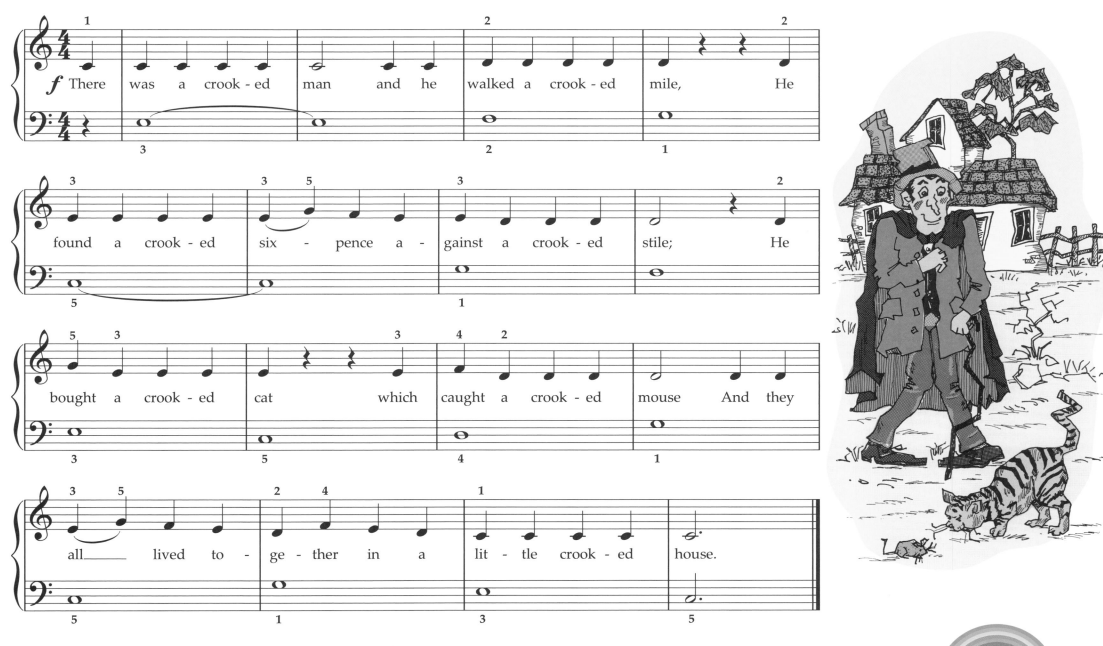

## Footsteps in the snow

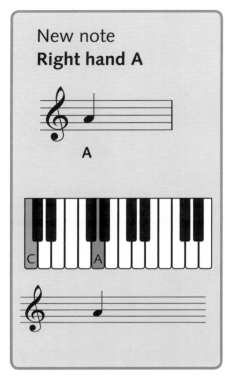

New note
**Right hand A**

A

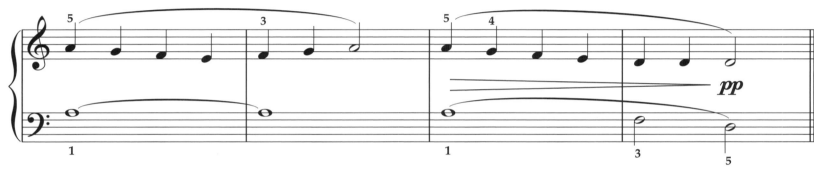

*pp* = *pianissimo* = **very soft**

# Twinkle, twinkle, little star

# Rain, rain, go away

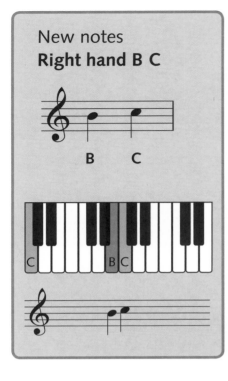

Rain, rain, go a - way, Come a - gain a - no - ther day.

Rain, rain, go to Spain, Ne - ver show your face a - gain.

*ff* = *fortissimo* = **very loud**

# My shadow

*Words by Robert Louis Stevenson*

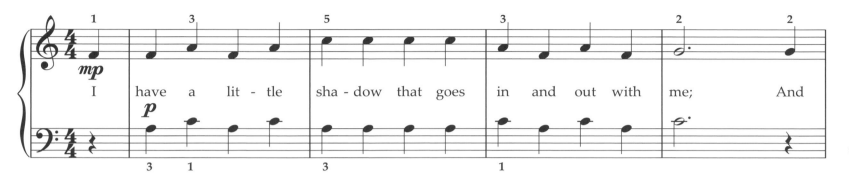

I have a lit - tle sha - dow that goes in and out with me; And

what can be the use of him is more than I can see.

## Musical detective

1 Which hand is the shadow, and why?
2 How many Cs does the right hand play?
3 How many Fs does the left hand play?

New rhythm
**Quaver (eighth note)**

♪

1 **quaver** looks like this: ♪ or ♩

2 quavers look like this: ♫ or ♫

4 quavers look like this: ♫♫

♫  ♩

2 quavers = one crotchet

**Remember** 1 crotchet = 1 beat

Clap this rhythm, saying the words aloud:

Baa - baa   black   sheep,   have you  a - ny wool?

Yes   sir,   yes   sir,   three   bags   full.

One   for the mas - ter and   one   for the dame,

One   for the lit - tle boy who  lives   down the lane.

# Turkey in the straw

# The mouse

# Lightly row

$\frac{3}{8}$ means 3 quaver beats in a bar.

A quaver rest looks like this:

# Umbrellas

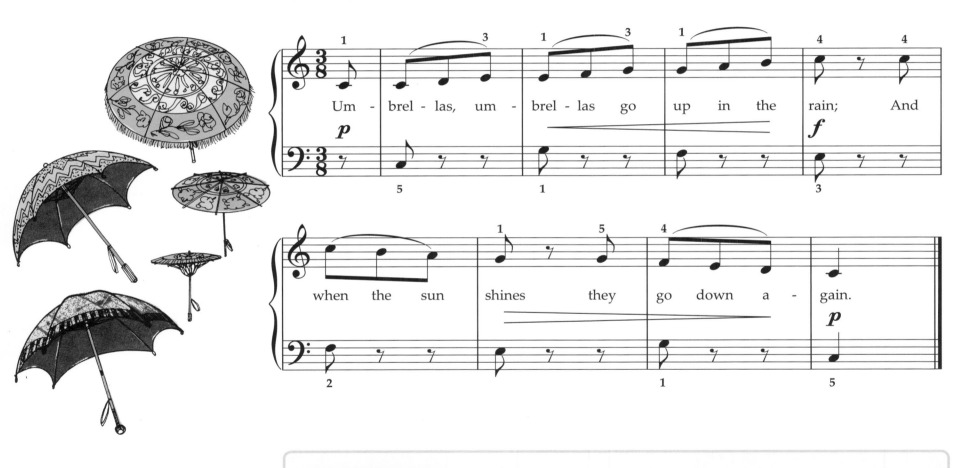

Um - brel - las, um - brel - las go up in the rain; And
when the sun shines they go down a - gain.

**Some Italian terms (speed)**

*Andante* = **at a walking pace**

*Moderato* = **at a moderate speed**

*Allegretto* = **fairly quick, but unhurried**

*Allegro* = **quick and bright**

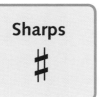

## Sharps

#

When you see this sign ♯ in front of a note, you must play the **black note** immediately above. This sign is called a **sharp**.

Play these **right-hand** notes, naming them aloud:

Now play these **left-hand** notes, naming them aloud:

Here's a tune all on **black notes**. Use the third finger of each hand to play alternate notes.

## Black key study

When you see this sign at the beginning of a line it means **F** is always **sharp**.
This is called a **key signature**.

## To market

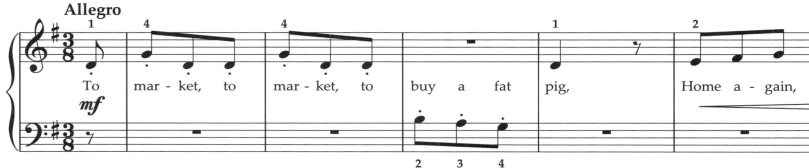

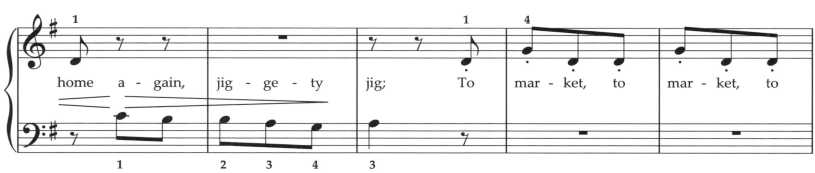

## Yankee Doodle *duet*

*Primo* = **higher pianist**
*Secondo* = **lower pianist**

Later on you can learn
the secondo part.

# Monkey puzzles 1

**1  Trace over these clefs then copy some more:**

**2  Name these notes:**

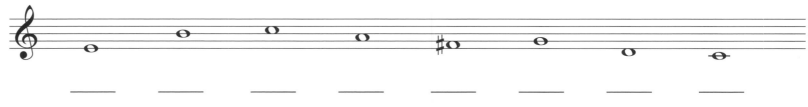

**3  Write these notes on the stave:**

| minim G | quaver B | semibreve F♯ | crotchet D | dotted minim A |

| crotchet D | semibreve G | quaver C | minim B | dotted minim F♯ |

**4** How many beats are there in each of these rests?

_____    _____    _____    _____

**5** Write the key signature of G major:

**6** How many crotchets are there in a dotted minim?    _____

How many minims are there in a semibreve?    _____

How many quavers are there in a crotchet?    _____

How many crotchets are there in a semibreve?    _____

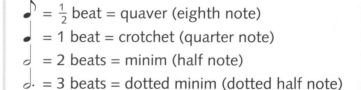

♪ = ½ beat = quaver (eighth note)
♩ = 1 beat = crotchet (quarter note)
𝅗𝅥 = 2 beats = minim (half note)
𝅗𝅥. = 3 beats = dotted minim (dotted half note)
𝅝 = 4 beats = semibreve (whole note)

**7** Add the barlines to these two tunes:

## Flats

♭

When you see this sign ♭ in front of a note, you must play the **black note** immediately below.
This is called a **flat**.

## J'ai du bon tabac *duet*

### Secondo

*Old French*

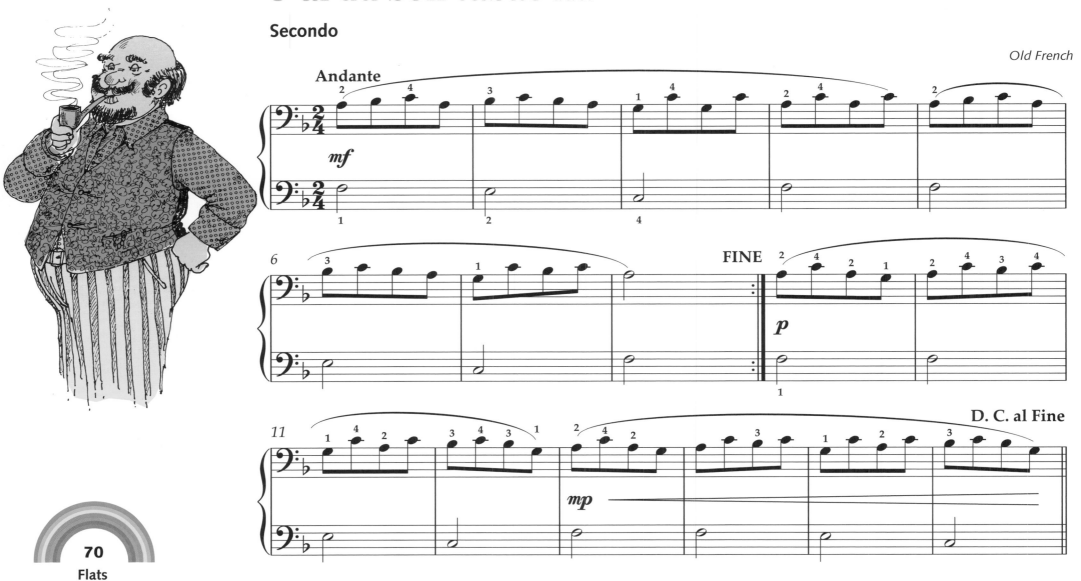

**New key F major**

This is the key signature of **F major**.
It means **B** is always **flat**.

# J'ai du bon tabac *duet*

**Primo**

Play both hands one octave higher.

*Old French*

**D.C. al fine**
Go back to the beginning and play until you reach **Fine** (the end).

New key F major

# William Tell Overture

Rossini

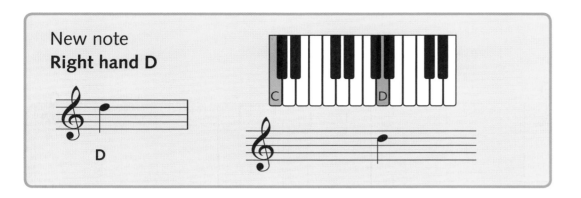

New note
**Right hand D**

D

Two notes slurred together like this are called a **couplet**.

Drop down on the first note, and spring up lightly on the second.

# Post-horn galop

Allegro

## Musical detective

1  How many couplets are there?
2  Does the piece get louder or softer?
3  How many bars have repeated notes only?

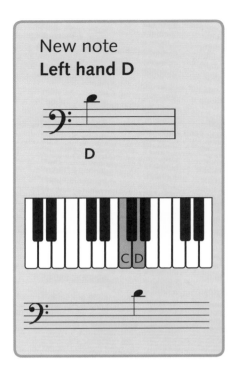

New note
**Left hand D**

D

# Cuckoo

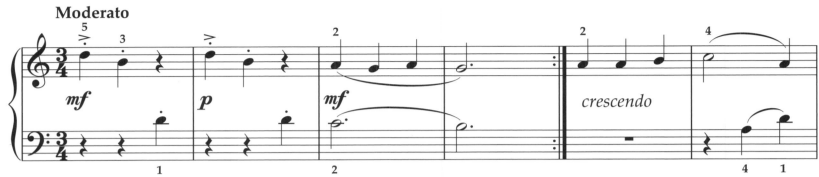

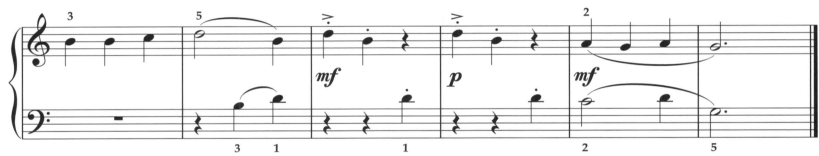

**Musical detective**

How many times can you hear the cuckoo?

# Happy birthday *duet*

Fill in your name in bar 6.

**Primo**

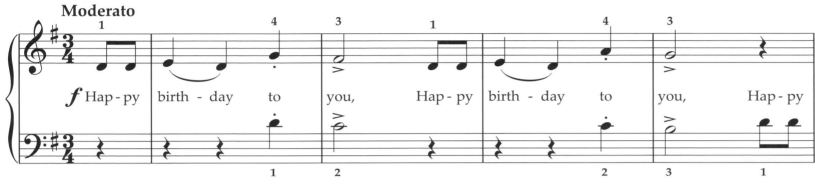

**Secondo**

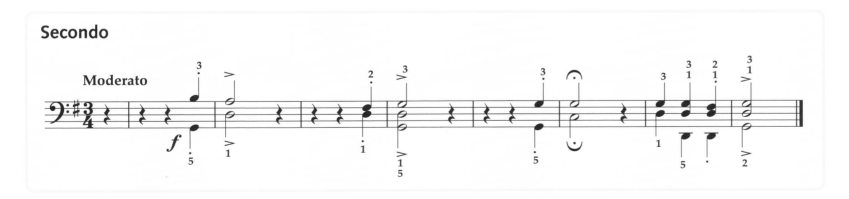

# Katie's waltz *duet*

**Secondo**

*Sim. (simile)* = **continue playing in the same way**

**Allegretto grazioso**

**76**

Katie's waltz

# Katie's waltz *duet*

Play both hands one octave higher.

**Primo**

*Allegretto grazioso*

*Grazioso* = **gracefully**

New rhythm
**Dotted crotchet
(dotted quarter note)**

𝅘𝅥. = dotted crotchet = 𝅘𝅥 + 𝅘𝅥𝅮

# Bonfire night

Con brio = **brightly**

Con brio

Ro - ckets and | Cath -'rine Wheels, | Spark -lers and | Jump - ing Jacks | Light up the

sky, What a | glo - ri - ous | sight! | Sand -wich - es, | sau - sa - ges,

Hot dogs and | crun - chy sticks | Make such a | feast on a | cold win - ter's | night.

**78**

Dotted crotchet

# Bobby Shaftoe

This sign ♮ is called a **natural**, and it cancels a sharp or a flat.
**Sharps**, **flats** and **naturals** not in the key signature are called **accidentals**.

This rhythm

sounds like this:

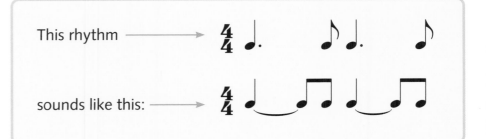

## The muffin man

Clap the rhythm of the right hand before you play.

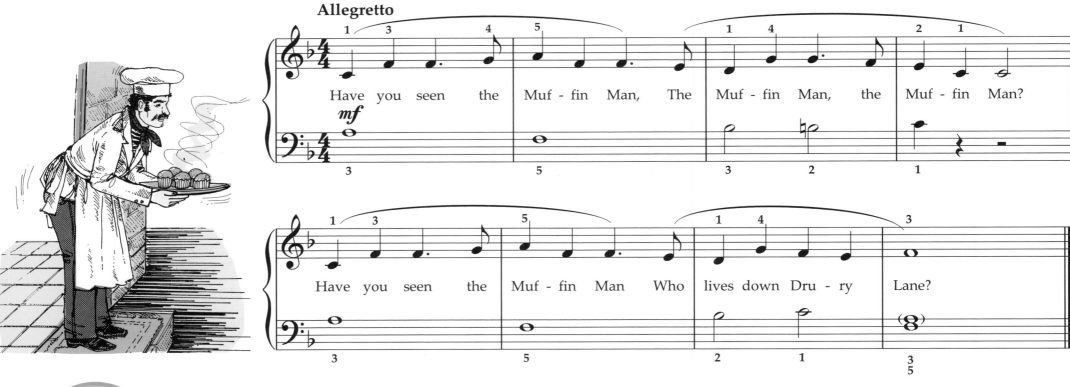

**Allegretto**

Have you seen the Muf - fin Man, The Muf - fin Man, the Muf - fin Man?

*mf*

Have you seen the Muf - fin Man Who lives down Dru - ry Lane?

# Rock-a-bye baby

**Andante**

Rock - a-bye ba - by on the tree - top. When the wind

*p dolce*

blows the cra - dle will rock. When the bough breaks the

cra - dle will fall, Down will come ba - by, cra - dle and all.

*Dolce* = **softly and sweetly**

# Monkey puzzles 2

**1  Write these notes:**

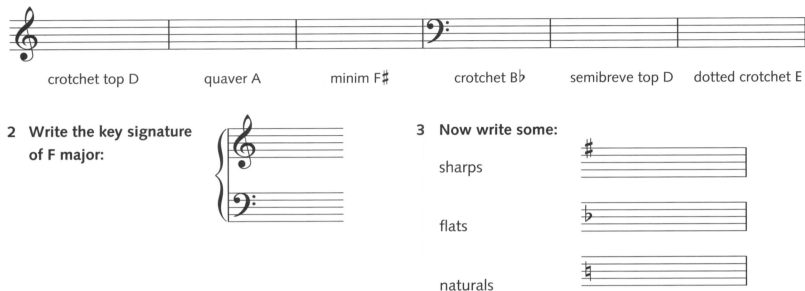

crotchet top D    quaver A    minim F♯    crotchet B♭    semibreve top D    dotted crotchet E

**2  Write the key signature of F major:**

**3  Now write some:**

sharps

flats

naturals

**4  Mark the B♭s in this piece:**

Deck    the hall    with    boughs    of    hol - ly,    Fa  la  la  la  la,    la    la    la    la

**5  Finger these pieces. Do you recognise the tunes?**

**6 Use the music notes to write in the missing letters to make these sentences:**

Mozart's ___ ___ ___ taught him to pl ___ y musi ___ ___ t ___ n

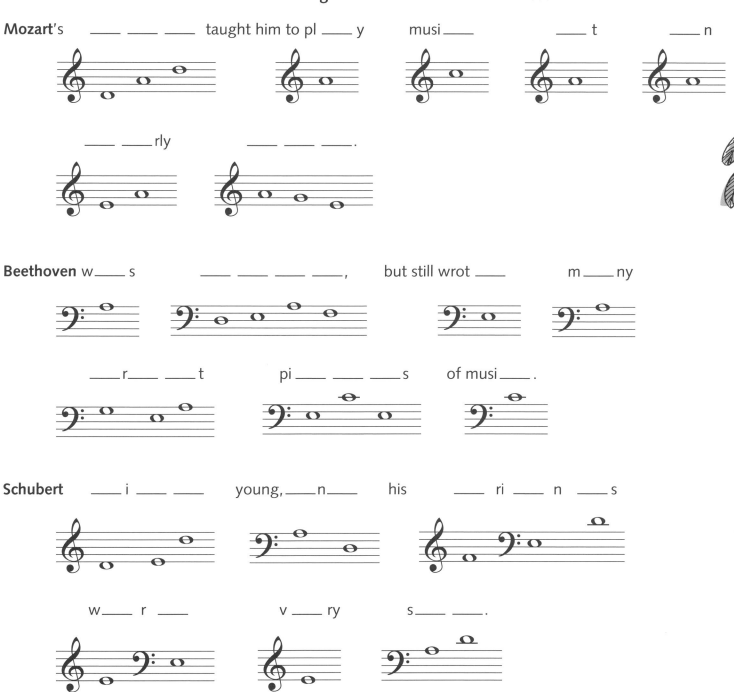

___ ___ rly ___ ___ ___ .

Beethoven w ___ s ___ ___ ___ ___ , but still wrot ___ m ___ ny

___ r ___ ___ t pi ___ ___ s of musi ___ .

Schubert ___ i ___ ___ young, ___ n ___ his ___ ri ___ n ___ s

w ___ r ___ v ___ ry s ___ ___ .

## Intervals

An **interval** is the distance between two notes.

Play these intervals:

Second    third    fourth    fifth    sixth    seventh    octave

## Chopsticks

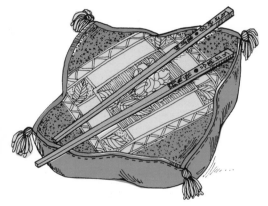

### Musical detective

How many different intervals can you find in this piece?

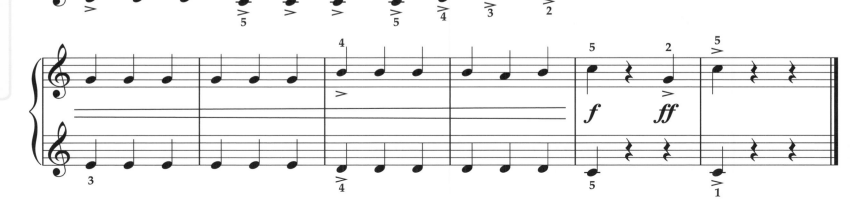

Two or more notes played together make a **chord**.

Footsteps coming:

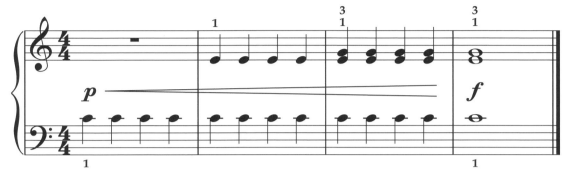

Footsteps going:

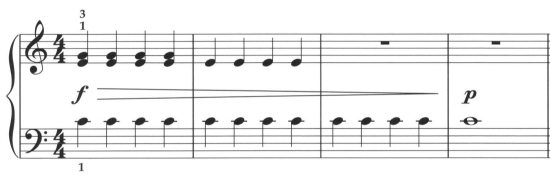

Footsteps coming and going:

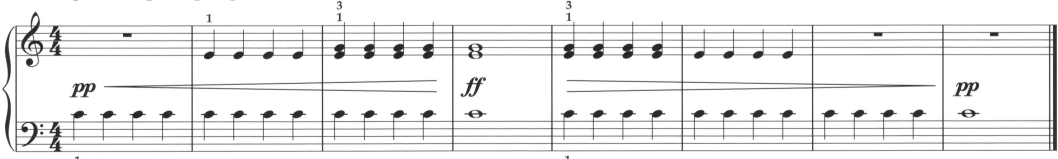

Remember: *pp* — *p* *mp* *mf* *ff* *mf* *mp* *p* — *pp*

# War drums

# Moon and stars waltz

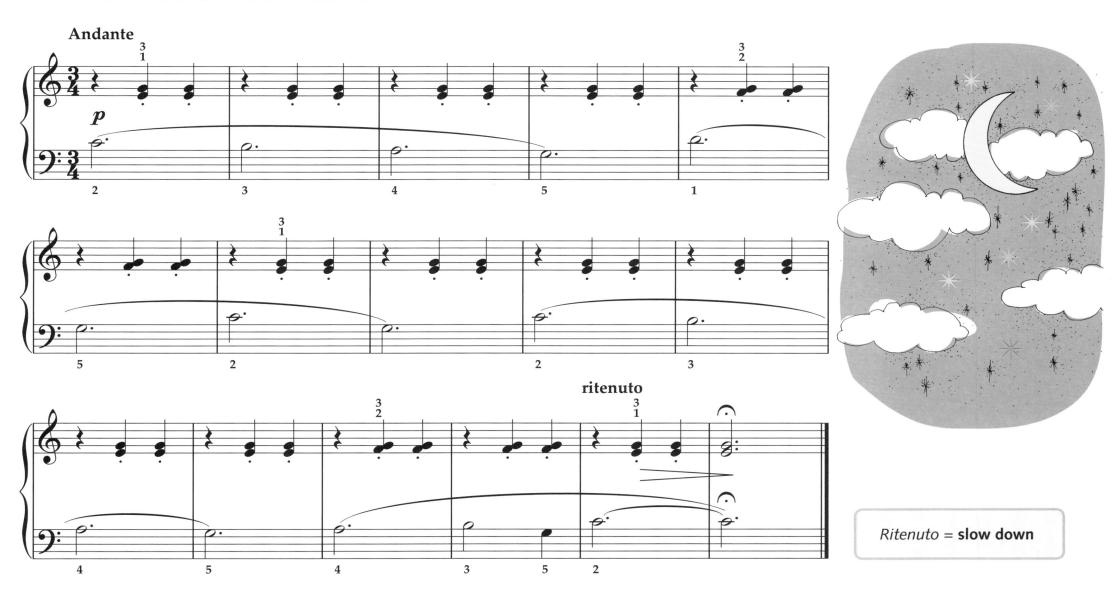

*Ritenuto* = **slow down**

## Musical detective

1  The moon is gliding in the sky and the stars are sparkling. Which hand is the moon and which is the stars?
2  Name the intervals in the right hand chords.

# The fairground

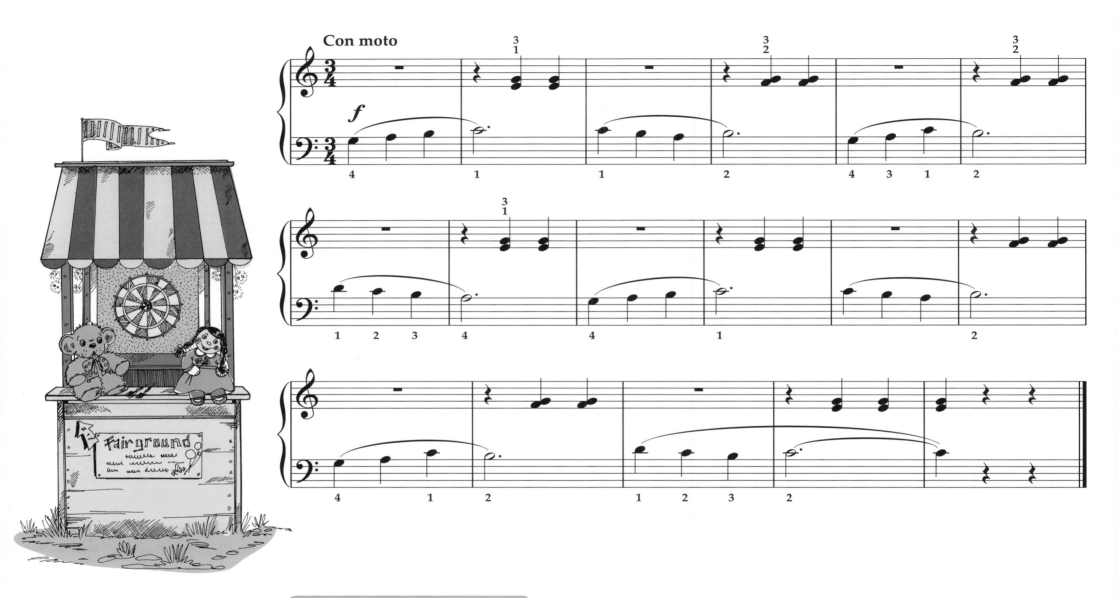

Con moto

*f*

Con moto = **moving along**

# Can can

Offenbach

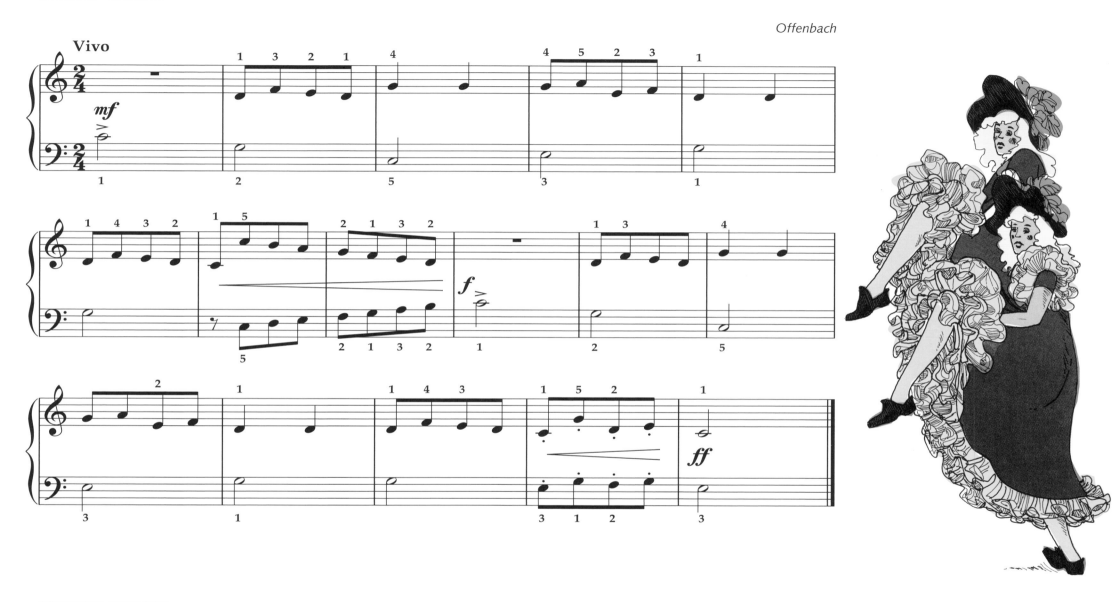

Vivo

mf

f

ff

Vivo = lively

# I'm a little teapot

# Three blind mice

New notes
**Left hand G  A**
**B**

Allegro

Three blind mice,___ Three blind mice,___

See how they run,___ See how they run,___ *mf* They

all ran af - ter the far - mer's wife, Who cut off their tails with a carv - ing knife, *f* Did

ev - er you see such a thing in your life, As three blind mice?___

New notes LH G, A, B

# There was a young lady from Niger

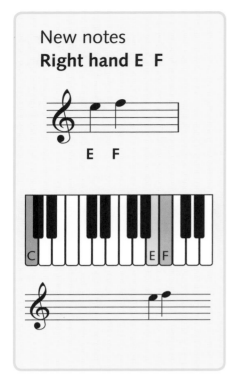

New notes
**Right hand E F**

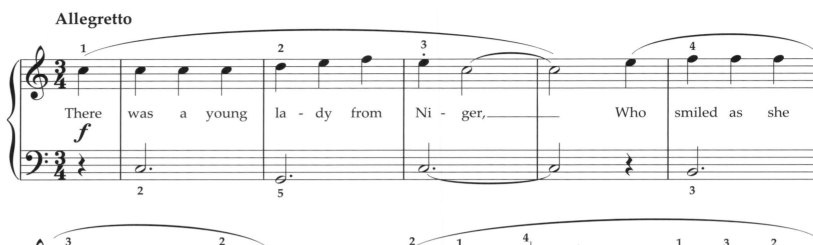

**Allegretto**

There was a young la - dy from Ni - ger, Who smiled as she

*f*

rode on a ti - ger, They came back from the ride With the

*p* *cresc.*

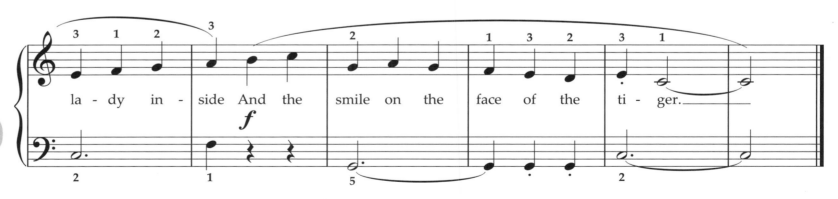

la - dy in - side And the smile on the face of the ti - ger.

*f*

# The musical ladder

All the notes you have learnt:

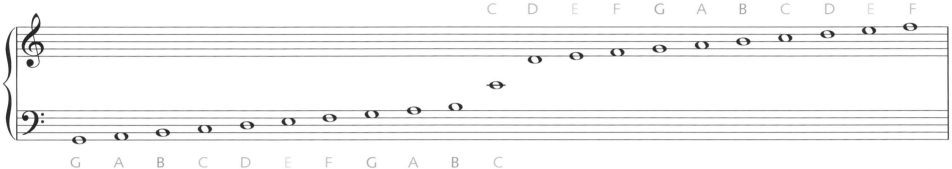

C D E F G A B C D E F

G A B C D E F G A B C

## Lines

### Treble clef

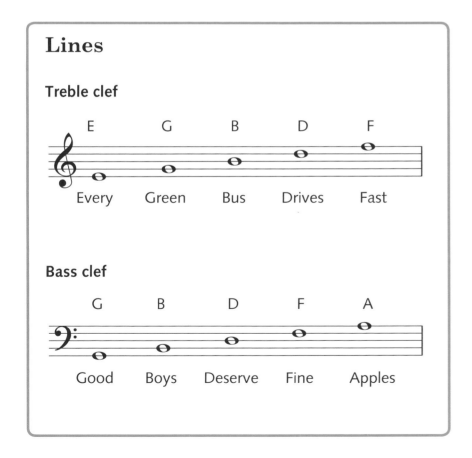

E     G     B     D     F

Every  Green  Bus  Drives  Fast

### Bass clef

G     B     D     F     A

Good  Boys  Deserve  Fine  Apples

## Spaces

### Treble clef

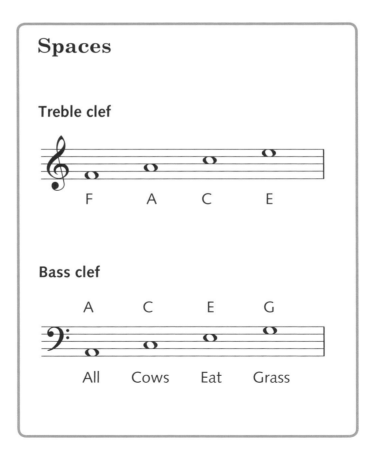

F     A     C     E

### Bass clef

A     C     E     G

All  Cows  Eat  Grass

# The grasshopper and the elephant

*Bucalossi*

*Leggiero = **lightly***

## Musical detective

This piece has lots of accidentals. Put a pencil cross over all the ones you can find.

# God save the Queen

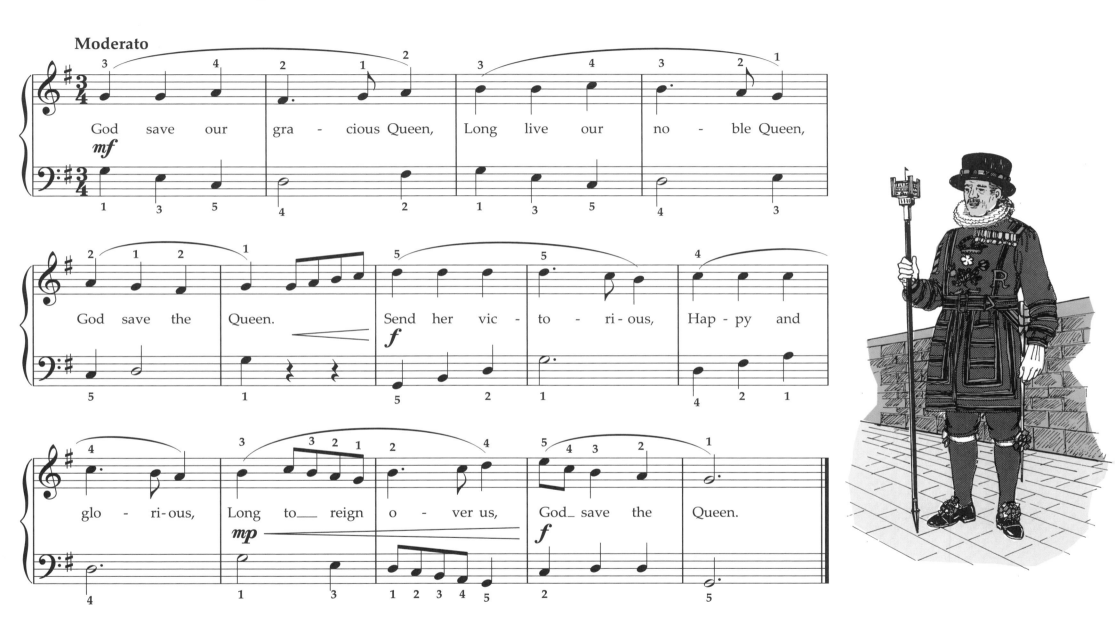

God save our gra - cious Queen, Long live our no - ble Queen,

God save the Queen. Send her vic - to - ri - ous, Hap - py and

glo - ri - ous, Long to reign o - ver us, God save the Queen.

# Rainbow certificate

This is to certify that

_____

successfully completed

## Me and My Piano Part 2

on _____

## Congratulations!

*Fanny Waterman.*

*Fanny Waterman*

*Marion Harewood*

*Marion Harewood*

_____

*Teacher's signature*